To Dionne Codrington

'Together we do better for the Kingdom of God
For divided we fall, but united we stand'

Contents

Introduction

Part 1: Definitions

Part 2: Hebrew Economic Laws

Part 3: Economic Preliminaries

Introduction

Here I, a servant of the LORD from my youth, provide a
report of my investigations which I have done on the matter of
debt. I have traversed both the academic and professional
worlds at times of peace and turmoil. I must now, at this time,
share the wisdom I have been endowed with those upon the
earth who are grappling with great challenges in the world of
economics and finance – a world which can be harmonised by
law.

This treatise provides the theoretical foundation to understand
the essential links between the real and financial sectors of the
economy, which are one, if harmonised according to biblical
principles. The parabolic nature of biblical law and economic
principles allow this.

The knowledge contained here provides an explanation of
how circular functions, in particular Pi, can be generalised to
explain the debt in a macroeconomic framework. The links
between the goods sector and financial sector are expounded

in a way so as to highlight why debt crises are endemic unless divine law is adhered to.

Harmony, my friends.

Part 1: Definitions

i. Agents, creditors, and debtors

Agents are economic actors. In this treatise there are only two types of agents: creditors and debtors. Agents can represent individuals; a coalition of individuals; or nations. Each agent can either be a creditor or a debtor in any distinct period. These roles naturally reverse in the eventuality of a debtor paying off their debts - in a two period scenario the creditor would transform into the debtor in the second period and vice versa.

ii. Asymmetric and symmetric wealth

Now I define two types of wealth: symmetric and asymmetric. A change to symmetric wealth leaves the relative position of the agents constant. Symmetric wealth implies that the agents in an economic system do not require debt instruments: all agents can fund their purchases in the goods – spot - market without recourse to credit markets due to the fact their outputs generate precisely the income required to meet their outgoings. Asymmetric wealth, however, implies that the relative positions are altered and hence debt instruments are required at the instance of the change in asymmetric wealth.

iii.   Production and output

Production represents the quantity of goods or services which an agent can produce given their – assumed fixed – factors of production. In contrast, output defines the quantity of goods and services actually sold in a market, that is to say, sold for a price.

Part 2: Hebrew Economic Laws

i.   No theft Commandment

In the twentieth chapter of the book Exodus and the fifteenth verse, the King James Version of the bible reads: "Thou shalt not steal". This is the second of the economic commandments. This is fundamental to the workings of a market economy; the underpinning of the principle of the protection of property rights. This implies that any interactions in a market economy must be mutually advantageous to those engaging in the interaction. As such, in equilibrium, the interaction results in merely changes to symmetric wealth. This engages the fundamental principle that one is to love their neighbour as their own self as any trade is not to alter their relative wealth – vis-à-vis one another – but rather leave both with equal benefit and cost from the transaction.

ii. Sabbath Commandment

In the twentieth chapter of the book of Exodus and the eighth verse until the eleventh verse, the bible reads: "Remember the sabbath day, to keep it holy. Six days shalt thou labour, and do all thy work: But the seventh day is the sabbath of the LORD thy God: in it thou shalt not do any work, thou, nor thy son, nor thy daughter, thy manservant, nor thy maidservant, nor thy cattle, nor thy stranger that is within thy gates: For in six days the LORD made heaven and earth, the sea, and all that in them is, and rested the seventh day: wherefore the LORD, blessed the sabbath day, and hallowed it."

This commandment allows a synchronised engagement of agents with the market economy. Six-sevenths of potential working hours were to be actually engaged in over a given week – ignoring other rest days stipulated throughout the year. As days are scaled to years, this has the implication that six out of seven years are spent in days of labour. Moreover, as we traverse one week of seven days, we can envision this commandment of allowing one day of rest to occur for every six days of work.

iii. Debt laws

In the fifteenth chapter of Deuteronomy and the first verse until the third the bible reads: "At the end of every seven years thou shalt make a release. And this is the manner of the release: every creditor that lendeth ought unto his neighbour shall release it; he shall not exact it of his neighbour; because it is called the LORD's release. Of a foreigner thou mayest exact it again: but that which is thine with thy brother thine hand shall release."

This verse dictates that the debt cycle was to occur over seven years but at the end of the seventh year the debt cycle was to cease. One should note that in this time period, six years of interactions in the goods market will have occurred. Hence, the ratio of the goods market interaction to the financial market interaction is to be six-sevenths.

In the book of Leviticus and the twenty fifth chapter and the eighth verse until the eleventh the bible reads: " And thou shalt number seven Sabbaths of years unto thee, seven times seven years and the space of the seven Sabbaths of years shall be unto thee forty and nine years. Then shalt though cause the trumpet of the jubilee to sounds on the tenth day of the seventh month, in the day of atonement shall ye make the trumpet sound throughout all your land. And ye shall hallow the fiftieth year, and proclaim liberty throughout all the land unto all the inhabitants thereof: it shall be a jubilee unto you: and ye shall return every man unto his possession, and ye shall return every man unto his family. A jubilee shall that fiftieth year be unto you: ye shall not sow, neither reap that which groweth of itself in it, nor gather the grapes in it of thy vine undressed."

In the book of Deuteronomy and the twenty third chapter and the nineteenth verse unto the twentieth, the bible reads: "Thou shalt not lend upon usuary to thy brother; usuary of money, usuary of victuals, usuary of any thing that is lent upon usuary: Unto a stranger thou mayest lend upon usuary; but unto thy brother thou shalt not lend upon usuary: that the LORD thy God may bless thee in all that thou settest thin hand to in the land whither thou goest to possess it."

This verse implies that Israelites were not to lend at interest to a fellow Isralite but could do to foreigner. This meant that any given Isralite could lend at interest but borrow for free from their fellow Israelite.

Part 3: Economic Preliminaries

The nature of spot market economy

A market economy has three key characteristics that are of importance. Firstly, the commandment not to steal must be upheld, meaning that agents' rights to their property are respected, and if not, they are protected. Secondly, money is used to purchase goods. This can be obtained by holding collateral at a central bank or else a government 'creating' claims over resources. Thirdly, any transaction, in equilibrium, should result in asymmetric wealth being unchanged but with a non-negative increase in symmetric wealth.

Any given transaction in a market must leave those agents in a 'flat' position or else, in the presence of perfect knowledge, they would not both mutually consent to that transaction. Hence, any market transaction should leave agents 'flat'.

ii. The nature of debt finance

Debt finance, however, leads to a change in asymmetric wealth. In the presence of positive real interest rates, this change in asymmetric wealth must advantageous to the creditor. This is why borrowers are servant to lenders.

Consider an economy of two agents, which can be each respectively constructed of individuals or any coalition of individuals. In a spot market economy, by which I mean an economy where every transaction is settled instantaneously - without option of recourse to credit - the output of these two agents must be equal at all times. In any dynamic framework, by which I mean a framework that permits credit this constraint must still hold over any specified time period whereby debt equates to zero by the end of the period.

There a two factors that determine a given agents command over resources. Firstly, the general level of production, and, secondly, the relative purchasing power of an agent: the availability and the means.

The advantage of debt finance is that agents can transfer the responsibility of production over any two periods. This means that they can respond to asymmetric shocks, which even out over time, in a way that allows each to bear all or a disproportionate amount of the production burden, for any given level of joint output, so long as this process is reflected in a mirror: their relative position inversed. This means that so long as the agents, in the second period, exchange their production burdens, debt is zero at the end.

Debt cannot change the joint level of production but it allows the agents' mean levels of production to be equal over the total time period whilst allowing their instantaneous production levels, in each of the two periods, be different but the inverse of the other agents in the other period.

iii.   Implications

Once a debt transfer has been enacted, this leads to an alteration of asymmetric wealth. However, agents are then referred to the goods market to generate the necessary changes in surpluses to achieve this. The problem is that the goods market is such that wealth remains symmetric under all transactions - in a perfect knowledge equilibrium.

The implied solution is that for a debt cycle to be resolved external factors must even out between the agents over the given time period of analysis. Hence, debt is to be merely used as an insurance mechanism rather than a speculative process as any shock must be symmetric. This is because, if debt were used by a debtor for investment purposes, they could not hold the same expectations as the creditor as if they profited from this transaction, this would lead to an increase in their asymmetric wealth. As such, this would be to the disadvantage of the creditor. Hence, this process would be required to be dependent upon creditors and debtors holding incompatible beliefs about the economy in equilibrium i.e. perpetual imperfect and asymmetric information.

Hence, the only mutually compatible incentive to have debt is to mutually mange external shocks so as to maximise - keep to the brim - production levels and therefore to keep unemployment to a minimum. Hence, the purpose of debt is to maximise symmetric wealth whilst keep asymmetric wealth constant. This is because agents must interact in any market by mutual consent. Hence, no market can transfer asymmetric wealth as no rational agent would mutually consent to having their position weakened with respect to the position of another agent with whom they compete for resources.

Part 4: Mathematical economic framework

i. Pi: linear to circular mapping

The key mathematical function used here is the circular operator Pi. This allows one to map a linear space into a circular one: a semi-circle.

The extent of production of agents can be measured by x and y axes – as measured from the origin. For now, we assume that the two agents have a fixed joint ability to produce goods and services i.e. a fixed amount of factors of production that allow a normalised maximum of one - a linear length of the radius one - to be produced.

Debt can be modelled by Pi i.e. the first quadrant of a circle representing the different equivalent Euclidean spaces (of length one – the radius - that result of the agents sharing production responsibility between them. This would then need to be mirrored in the fourth quadrant of a circle - with production responsibilities being reversed. However, I now proceed to introduce money into this framework.

Given that the agents are faced with a monetary market their maximum outputs must be half of their production levels as half must be used to obtain cash money i.e. held at a central bank type institution as collateral. Thus far, the money market is unsettled and money can continue to be an outstanding liability.

An alternative way to model this outcome is that the cord connecting the orthogonal x and y axes at points of where the respective axes are of length one. This represents linear combinations of the two maximum production levels. As we move from the tip of the east radius towards the tip of north radius - along this cord - this represents agent one producing increasingly of the joint output potential of one until agent two is responsible for all of the production. However, in a spot market, final output levels must be equal and this means that final output settles at a point of a half each – half the radius. This occurs as we know that total output achievable is one and hence they must settle at a half each as the increase output in any given of the agents respective output spaces impacts on the other in a fashion akin to a zero sum game.

The Pi operator allows their joint Euclidean spaces to remain constant. Debt transfers cannot change the Euclidean space of economic activity between agents, and hence the debt space can be modelled by the Pi operator. If production of the least productive agent is one, then the maximum joint output, if purchases happen in a monetary market simultaneously, then the maximum joint output is one. This represents interdependent production levels, which equate to the maximum achievable joint output given this 'monetary constraint' – the constraint that a spot market requires output levels to be equalised. Each individual can achieve an output of a half.

ii. A Hebrew seven circle theorem: the optimal construction of circular space and debt

Consider that the minimum economic space is circular. Any optimum space must be circular as it represents the most efficient way to hold a given amount of space. If this represents a standard building block then we have to consider how to construct a larger space with units of the size of this initial circular space. The new optimum space of the next step of a scale upwards would be to adjoin six equivalent circles to the outside of this in a way that that each is tangential to the centre circle and each is also tangential to two other circles. This would be a construction of seven circles. This means that, if one connects six circles in the manner of the outer six circles there is left a space internally for a seventh.

We could then draw a circle around these seven to make a circle of area that is nine times the original sized circle – or nine pi - assuming a radius of one. This larger circle can be constructed by merely joining seven time seven circles – forty-nine together in a way akin to the initial seven. By doing this we encircle the middle seven to make a circle of nine pi in area, whilst maintaining the other forty-two units in their amalgamated state. This leads to a circularisation of a circular space.

The means that, over a period of forty-nine units, a larger unit of seven circles can be approximated as a circle of radius three. This increases the normalised activity space by two, from seven pi to nine pi. Hence, by using the sabbatical circle construction projector - ז - Hebrew for seven - this allows one to be generate a space whereby the debt cycle can unfold as this requires a space equivalent to three times the static production level achievable in one period and six times the output.

The circularisation of the circular space results in is achievable by ז because it optimises the unit space in it's interior whilst ensuring a symmetric and connected exterior, which are properties of the base unit.

Over forty-nine periods, new space then becomes fifty-one pi. However, in the process of construction i.e. if each unit represented a unit of time in a continuous time sequence, only forty-nine periods amalgamated. Thus, in the context of infinite space, made of units of forty-nine, these forty-nine units average out to be fifty, if this space is circularised and constructed optimally. In the infinity prior to the final optimised forty-nine circles the space is forty-nine. But once amalgamated, for proceeding infinity the space is fifty-one – which leads to an average of fifty in the limit of infinite time.

Seven circle debt theorem.

If economic activity can be modelled by the radius of a circle and it's orthogonal positive counterpart this means that debt space must be equivalent to this circle of radius three. This is because at the limit, at any one time, if an output is to be equivalent to one – as a joint output between the two agents – at any one point, whilst one agent is in total debt to the other, this must be so. This is because a joint normalised output of one by the two agents must be funded by the creditor. As such, the creditor must produce both the production level of one and then an additional one to use to exchange for money to purchase this output. This is then loaned out. However, in addition to this, the money is a claim on future output of this amount - one. And hence, in the limit, this implies a present value production of one. And so the total implied present value amount is three. However, for the agents to settle this in the future, the debtor must also produce an equivalent to three. This must occur because at any one point the creditor must also provide the future claimable amount in the static present. Hence, if a production of one is the maximum potential production level in a period of one, it takes six equivalent periods in total to produce enough between the debtor and creditor to settle this process. However, mathematically, the optimum connected space obtainable from six circular units allows a seventh unit, which is traversed by merit of traversing the six outer units, which are periods.

Intuitively, if debt is allowable, which it is in a monetary economy, this allows the activity space to be expanded to seven pi, at a maximum, when only six pi worth of output activity being conducted. Therefore any debt disequilibrium needs to be resolved within seven years for every six years of output production; of instantaneous settlement.
Hence, the ratio of discreet to continuous activity is six sevenths.

Part 5: Mathematical economic proofs

i.   Proof of Sabbath commandment

Pi maps out a space where there is no monetary constraint (that output levels must be equal at all points within the time period) but joint production levels are maximised. However, the monetary constraint is that output is a half of independent output.

Understanding the role of seven periods with respect to one period

Assume that the money market is resolved - funded - within a given period. We make this period unity. This means that if a space is one then the monetary constraint allows an output of a half.

When considering agents acting independently this can be viewed mathematically as orthogonality – agent one is a perpendicular projection from the origin of agent two's position and vice versa. One can measure each individual's output as their vertical (horizontal for agent one) distance from the origin.

Considering agent two – the y-axis - if this vertical line is rotated, even in the least, this can be viewed as the agent contributing to the benefit of the other whilst hindering their own utility. As such, total sacrifice would entail a rotation of one fourth of pi.

The royal commandment is that we are to love our neighbour as ourselves. If both agents make an equal adjustment to the benefit of the other we end up on the forty-five degree line projection from the origin: northeast.

At this point the agent's outputs are equal and hence no borrowing is required. This maximises the individual distances from the origin of each individual – when considered from the perspective of their original orthogonal states. The intuition for this is that lending lowers output levels as some production is used for money – liquidity – and not output. Indeed, by co-ordinating production/ output levels we can economise when moving away from the origin. i.e. we can give up the minimum amount of production to use for monetary purchases by travelling both distances at once.

This is a mathematical example of two becoming one to each individual's advantage – together we do better. This epitomises the benefits entailed by obeying laws and is a prerequisite for any optimal law – that it generates the maximum advantage for each individual, if the other individual also obeys. This advantage happens to be a fifth part of the original linear space, when the space is circularised through time.

Hence, the most one can get individually away from the origin is seven tenths of productive potentially. However, this extra fifth is productive potential generated by a pure, unsettled, debt process. Hence, this can only yield an extra tenth of production to applied to the market, which is output.

The mystery of how to produce more than when acting orthogonally is to use less money in exchange. This has to involve outputs being equalised and hence money is not being used for lending. But one cannot use one hundred per cent of production as this would involve bartering. Nevertheless, by moving in both directions, equally and simultaneously, maximum efficiency is achieved – both contribute to the others advancement to equal measure.

The Sabbath commandment and debt

Consider a circle. The vertical radius is the maximum potential production level of agent two. The perpendicular radius, which is orthogonal to agent two, measures the maximum potential production level of agent one, with whom the debt contracts are made.

The maximum output, however, for each agent is half the radius as a monetary market is used and hence half of produce must be used as collateral to obtain cash money which is used to purchase the goods. Hence, the cord connecting the maximum production levels measures a linear average. The mid-point measures the maximum output levels of each agent, which are identical by definition.

Pi maps at a loci of points which represent how the maximum joint output can be shared between them, if debt may be used i.e. agents are not constrained to produce output simultaneously but are required to trade in a monetary market. Given that output requires production levels to be equalised, the maximum point is where the forty-five degree line crosses the original cord - stretching out to the edge of the circle i.e. the radius at the forty-five degree line projection. This means that if debt can be utilised under the constraint of monetary settlements the maximum production is at sine forty-five and cosine forty-five, which results in orthogonal production levels of one divided by the square root of two, which is approximately seventh tenths.

Hence, the effect of utilising debt is to enlarge the space to approximately seven tenths of the maximum level of production. Hence, debt increases the base level of output from a half to approximately seven tenths.

However, this augmentation of two-fifths must also be settled in a monetary market and hence only one fifth can be added to the original orthogonal production levels. And hence, the final resultant maximum level of output is six-tenths of maximum production. However, this is only determined post the debt settlement i.e. it is backed out from the debt augmented position and hence debt operates over seven-tenths, whilst output operates over six-tenths.

Hence, the Sabbath commandment allows these rhythms to be synchronised – the goods market and the financial market.

However, precision is required. The orthogonal lengths, when optimised, must square to yield a half. However, seven-tenths can be used in a circular framework, to sum to one half when squared. This is because if we square seven-tenths we obtain forty-nine hundred parts, which are circular by assumption. In an optimised circular framework this sums to fifty hundredths in an infinite time period.

However, over time, purchases can happen at distinct times. This allows the space of debt activity to be six times average yearly output level. Now all potential production of a given individual can be traded in a year. For this to occur six years of production is necessary. This allows one third of this to be used to purchase the production, a third to be used as cash to purchase this output, which now equals yearly joint output. However, this cash is a liability, which must be accounted for in a complete cycle of debt. This implies another third is taken up producing the output to 'pay-off' this liability. Hence, the output space for a year can be approximated by six years of equivalent space if this is to be transformed into a debt space.

ii.   Proof of debt law

The need of debt cancellation

If the debt process is not settled in over seven periods it implies that there is fundamental mismatch between the production possibilities of the two agents over the seven years and hence a larger cycle is required for settlement. This is to say that the shock that is causing the temporary mismatch is of a larger magnitude than a shock that balances out within a seven-year period.

Hence, the limit for a debt process is seven years. After that debt must be forgiven or else it cannot be resolved in a way compatible with the spot goods market.

Proof of zero interest rate law

In a spot market, output between two agents must be equal, which implies no unsettled debt cycle. Intertemporally, the spot result must hold– over any 'fixed' period of consideration, wealth must be symmetric over this fixed period. Hence, interest rates must be zero - or at least netted to zero - for this to hold. Indeed, given the necessary physical symmetry of a debt system interest rates must be zero if it is to be settled in a market economy, by mutual consent.

Proof one

If in the first period of a two period debt cycle there is debt, this implies that the borrower will need to generate an output surplus in the second period equivalent to the principal plus the real interest.

But, if there are only two agents, this surplus, over an above the first period's production, must be produced by generating disequilibrium in relative outputs equivalent to the interest rate. This would thereby put the creditor into debt in the second period. Hence, hypothetically, further periods would be required to settle the debt, which yields a fundamental problem. With positive real interest rates – or rather non-zero real net interest rates – this process would have to go on indefinitely as the surplus to be generated would continue to increase in monotonic fashion as the responsibility to generate this surplus shifted from back and forth between the agents over specified future time periods. Hence, interest rates must be driven to zero if a stable equilibrium is to hold.

This can only be achieved if interest rates are zero or savings (compression of consumption out of income) rise to infinity. However, savings too must be bounded by production levels. Hence, continuous and exponentially increasing growth would have to occur continuously and indefinitely

Proof two

In the spot market the relative output levels of the two agents must be equalised at all times over any fixed period. If there is a positive real interest rate, this implies that the output of one agent is greater than the other over this fixed period, to account for the real interest above the principal. However, if a debt cycle is to be resolved – settled - then going forward, if there is to be no more debt then the production levels of the two agents would then have to be equal in all subsequent periods. However, over all periods – the amalgamated larger period - this would imply that the two production levels were unequal, except if the real interest rate equals zero.

Proof three

If an agent is a borrower in the first of two periods, then they must pay back the principal plus the real interest. However, this must be generated in the goods market. But the goods market is a zero sum market with respect to asymmetric wealth i.e. it consists of price times quantity. But the debt market trades asymmetric wealth or just wealth (price times quantity). The goods market allows price and quantity to move inversely so as to keep wealth symmetric through time. However, debt markets work so as to generate changes in asymmetric wealth. The debt markets have an inverse/ mirror effect on creditors and debtors whilst spot markets have symmetric effects.

Moreover, in a debt market, if there is a change to the real interest rate, the effect on debt quantity demands and supplies is equivalent for the debtor vis-à-vis the creditor. An increase in interest rates leads to both want to save more i.e. both would ideally want to temporarily decrease their asymmetric wealth to achieve a permanent future increase. However, goods markets lead to opposite and equal decisions on the part of the interacting agents as regards their response to price changes.

In period two, the borrower, however, must generate a surplus in the goods market. But there is no wealth surplus (asymmetric) to be had as it is zero sum and agents are assumed to be behaving optimally. Hence, this can only be achieved if consumption is depressed by the debtor in period two, so as to generate the surplus, which is the real interest. This is achieved by increased saving - depressed consumption. This means that the adjustment has to be effected by a direct shift in asymmetric wealth rather than an incentivised shift. The increases in the interest rate merely serve to increase the adjustment required rather than incentivise the adjustment. Hence, whilst increases make it more difficult for the debtor to adjust, it cannot encourage them to save more, as to save more requires reducing consumption, which itself solves the problem directly and becomes merely an increased necessity to solve a now increased problem. Hence, it only serves to drive adjustment by increasing the pain. But then this pain would merely be shifted across to the creditor if solved.

Proof four

Moreover, interest rates should never be worthwhile for borrowers to bear. The only reason to borrow for a speculative purpose is to take advantage of a future expected increase in asymmetric wealth. However, a creditor cannot profit from this unless there is a positive interest rate, which yields an increase in their future asymmetric wealth. But if this is so, the borrower cannot increase their future asymmetric wealth (in equilibrium/ expectation) with perfect knowledge, by borrowing with interest rates, as the creditor would have no incentive to lend, if this were the mutually held expected outcome.

Conclusion

A general biblical principle

In the book of Numbers, in the fifth chapter and verses five through to seven, the bible reads:

" And the LORD spake unto Moses, saying, speak unto the children of Israel, When a man or woman shall commit any sin that men commit, to do a trespass against the LORD, and that person be guilty; then they shall confess their sin which they have done: and he shall recompense his trespass with the principal thereof, and add unto it the fifth part thereof, and give it unto him against whom he hath trespassed. "

It can be seen here that when a trespass of a law is made a fifth part of the principal lost is to be added in repayment. This makes logical sense because this recompenses from the societal loss due to the transgression.

The context used in this book is one of optimal rule setting – optimality of laws. The aim of a good law is to enhance the corporate and each sub-component of the corporate without demise to any individual or coalition of individuals. This can be distinguished from optimal individual choice. Optimal law setting is about the to the optimal choice of a judge; a ruler; a governor.

Man has power to enact laws of upon earth. These of interest to man as man can choose in this realm. God has given these economic laws so as to imbue harmony and goodness amongst men in their economic relations. When such laws are disobeyed, then naturally, we will have crises, which separate us.